D1492107

SEAS AND OCEANS

Design	David West
	Children's Book Design
Designer	Keith Newell
Editorial Planning	Clark Robinson Limited
Editors	Michael Flaherty
	Yvonne Ibazebo
Picture Researcher	Emma Krikler
Illustrator	Mike Saunders
Consultant	David Flint
	University lecturer

© Aladdin Books Ltd 1992
Designed and produced by
Aladdin Books Ltd
28 Percy Street
London W1P 9FF

First published in
Great Britain in 1992 by
Franklin Watts
96 Leonard Street
London EC2A 4RH

ISBN 0-7496-0805-6

A CIP catalogue record for this book is
available from the British Library.

Printed in Belgium

HANDS · ON · GEOGRAPHY

SEAS AND OCEANS

JOHN CLARK

GLOUCESTER PRESS
London · New York · Toronto · Sydney

CONTENTS

This book is all about the seas and oceans. The topics covered include how the oceans were formed millions of years ago, and how they are an important source of food and minerals. The book also tells you about the underwater landscape and the various plants and animals that live deep in the ocean depths. It explains how we can use the ocean's energy to generate electricity, and looks at ways in which the ocean is being polluted by mankind. There are "hands on" projects for you to do which use everyday items as equipment. There are also "did you know?" panels of information for added interest.

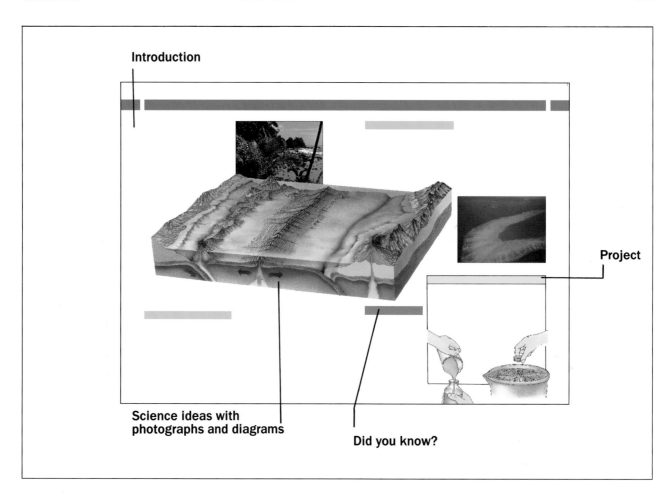

Introduction

Project

Science ideas with photographs and diagrams

Did you know?

Seas and oceans cover nearly three-quarters of the Earth's surface. Their waters are in constant motion because of powerful currents and tides. They are also home to thousands of different creatures, from shrimps and jellyfish to sharks and whales. The bottoms of the oceans are contoured by tall mountains, valleys and deep trenches. The sea bed is also constantly changing as molten rock from beneath the Earth's crust forces its way upwards, and old rocks sink back into the mantle. Volcanoes situated underwater also erupt, and help build new chains of islands.

Man has been interested in the seas and oceans for centuries. From the early explorations, using weighted rocks to measure the ocean depth, to today's modern vessels which can plunge all the way to the sea floor and examine the landscape.

This book describes the origin, composition and inhabitants of the oceans. It shows how the oceans can provide us with a rich source of food, mineral resources and energy. The book also explains how pollution, and other activities of mankind, may be putting these natural resources at risk.

Waves crashing into a huge rock in northern California's Pacific Ocean

Most of the Earth's surface is covered by the seas and oceans. This vast area of water — about 360 million square kilometres — surrounds the continents. When it is viewed from space, Earth appears as a blue planet with the continents appearing as occasional islands of brown land.

FORMATION

The Earth has not always been covered with water, and neither have the oceans always had their present shape. When the Earth first formed, it was a fiery ball of hot rock dotted with thousands of active volcanoes. As the volcanoes erupted, they emitted gases, mainly water vapour and carbon dioxide, into the atmosphere. In time the atmosphere became saturated with vapour and as the Earth cooled, it condensed and fell as rain. The volcanoes produced more and more steam, and so the cycle continued. Over millions of years, the rainwater accumulated on the surface, forming the seas and oceans of today.

During this early period, much of the land was joined together like a huge island. Then the continents separated and drifted to their present positions.

▽ Oceans on Earth began as steam from volcanoes, which condensed into rain clouds in the atmosphere. This rain gradually collected to form the world's oceans.

Water vapour and carbon dioxide

Forming atmosphere and oceans

Oceans

200 million yrs ago   **100 million yrs ago**   **50 million yrs ago**

SEA WATER

The oceans still get much of their water from rain. But the water does not just stay in the oceans, it is recycled. The Sun heats up the oceans and makes the water evaporate into the atmosphere as water vapour. As the vapour cools, it forms clouds which eventually release rain back to the Earth. The rain flows along rivers back into the sea.

The sea water also helps to regulate temperatures on land. The sea does not lose the sun's heat as fast as the land does. So during the cold winter months, breezes from the sea carry warm air to the land.

River water also washes various minerals into the sea. The most important one is salt (sodium chloride), which makes up an average of 3.5 per cent by weight of sea water. Other minerals in sea water include sulphates, magnesium, potassium and calcium; there are even small traces of gold in the sea. Sea water also contains dissolved oxygen, which is essential for the life of fish and other marine animals and plants.

▽ The world's oceans changed in size and shape as the continents slowly drifted apart. The Atlantic Ocean gets 3 centimetres wider every year.

Rain

Wind

Evaporation

△ The water cycle circulates water on Earth. Water evaporates from the oceans and forms clouds, which produce rain over the land.

▽ Water makes up 96.5 per cent of the sea. The rest consists of dissolved minerals, the most important being common salt.

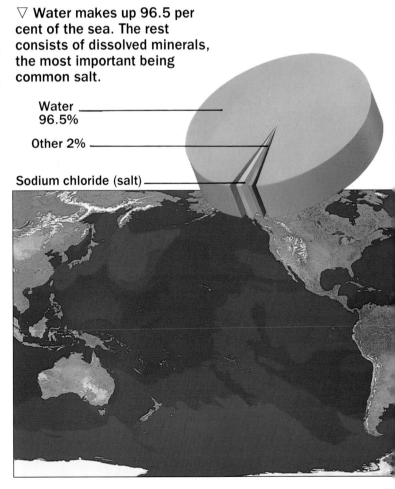

Water 96.5%

Other 2%

Sodium chloride (salt)

Present day

A satellite image of the Pacific Ocean

The oceans cover over 70 per cent of the Earth's surface, and have an average depth of 3,700 metres. Therefore, their waters provide the largest available space for living things. All marine plant life, and most animals, live in fairly shallow waters near the surface. But even the ocean depths have some life.

EVOLUTION

Life on Earth began in the ocean fringes. The sea consisted of a 'soup' of biochemicals which combined on rocks at the shore to form the first living cells. The first single-celled animals lived in the sea. These gradually evolved into multi-celled creatures without backbones, resembling the shellfish, worms and corals which live in the sea today.

Meanwhile, the green plants that had evolved on land helped to add oxygen to the Earth's atmosphere. The oxygen which dissolved in sea water became available to marine animals. The first animals to evolve with backbones were fish-like creatures called placoderms, whose bodies were covered in bony plates. These were also the ancestors of amphibians, the first backboned animals to move onto dry land. Fish continued to evolve in the sea, eventually giving rise to shark-like predators with skeletons made of cartilage and modern bony fish.

▽ The fish living in the oceans evolved over millions of years, from simple jellyfish to the more complex bony fish of today.

Coelacanth: a fish that dates back 300 million years

(1) Jellyfish (2) Mollusc
(3) Trilobite (4) Placoderm
(5) Rachitomes (6) First shark
(7) Birkenia (8) Modern shark
(9) Holostean (10) Modern fish

1200 million

1

900m

2

400m

3

4

500 million

5

300m

6

200m

7

9

8

10

LIVING IN WATER

Fish come in all shapes and sizes, from the small coral fish and sardines to the long, snake-like eels and huge basking sharks. And they have evolved various unique features to suit their life in the water. Fish have fins which they use to swim, and most have internal swim bladders that enable them to float in the water without sinking or rising to the surface. Cartilaginous fish such as the shark (right), have no swim bladders and sink if they stop swimming. All fish have gills which they use to extract oxygen dissolved in the sea. This allows them to 'breathe' under the water.

Fast-swimming fish have streamlined bodies that move easily through the water. For example, a 2 metre-long barracuda can swim at a speed of 12 metres a second (43 km/h) and turn in its own body length.

Tail fin

Second dorsal

Anal fin

Dorsal fin

Pelvic fin

Pectoral fin

Snout

Jaw

▽ Bony fish keep afloat by means of a swim bladder or air bladder. It is an elongated sac which contains air and lies above the digestive tract. The fish controls buoyancy by varying the amount and pressure of the air.

Swim bladder

MAKE A SWIM BLADDER

You can see how a fish's swim bladder works by making a model from a small bottle with a tight-fitting top. Fill a large bowl with water, half fill the bottle as well and screw on the top. Put the bottle in the bowl and see how it floats on the surface. Now gradually add more water to the bottle, screwing on the top and making it float each time. Eventually you will add the right amount of water for the bottle to just break the surface.

Bowl

Water

1/2 filled
3/4 filled

Each type of life form in the sea is found at a particular depth, from the shallow areas a few metres deep to the abyssal plain more than 4,000 metres deep. The amount of sunlight and the saltiness of the water, also determines the kind of plants and animals that are found at each ocean level.

THE CONTINENTAL SHELF

The continental shelf is the shallowest part of the sea. It starts at the edge of the continents and gently slopes downwards. The shelf is seldom more than 150 metres deep, and is also known as the euphotic zone. Because sunlight reaches the bottom of the shelf, seaweeds grow in this layer. The tiny animals near the surface, called zooplankton, consist of krill and other small shrimp-like crustaceans, as well as the eggs and young of various fish.

Apart from eating microscopic plants called phytoplankton, krill are a source of food for a range of marine creatures, from surface-feeding fish to baleen whales. Jellyfish also live near the surface, drifting with the currents and using the stinging cells in their tentacles to trap and kill small fish for food.

▽ The sea depth changes as you move away from land. Nearest the shore the sea is quite shallow. It tends to be deeper further out.

Land

Continental shelf

Continental slope

Continental rise

Abyssal plain

Sea level

Continental shelves extend round the edges of continents

▽ Starfish, crabs and other crustaceans live in the shallowest parts of the sea. Sharks sometimes visit these areas for food.

Green turtle

Dolphin

Jellyfish

Crab

White tip shark

Plankton

Mackerel

Angel fish

LIFE IN THE SHALLOWS

Most fish live in the shallow parts of the oceans, and end up feeding on each other. Small fish swim in shoals for protection, while predators such as barracuda and sharks swoop in to catch their prey. Other fish, such as conger eels, wait in rock crevices for their prey to swim within range. Flatfish scavenge on the bottom, quickly burying themselves in the sand or even changing colour when danger threatens.

Most of the predatory fish are active during the day. So at night, when it is less dangerous, other fish leave the deeper layers and swim upwards to feed in the shallows. Some of the plankton which live near the surface give off light, and so it is never completely dark, even at night. This light helps the night feeders to find food more easily.

Some inland lakes, such as the Caspian Sea and the Dead Sea, are so salty that they resemble shallow seas.

△ Although usually inhabitants of deeper water, white sharks swim into shallow water to feed. The large whale shark however, feeds only on plankton.

Salt crystals in the Dead Sea area

The layer of ocean water lying beyond the shallow surface is called the mesopelagic zone. It has a depth of about 2,000 metres. The bathypelagic is the next layer and it reaches all the way to the bottom, or ocean plain, with a depth of about 5,000 metres. No light penetrates either of these layers.

THE OCEAN PLAIN

The ocean plain is not a wide flat area, but consists of tall mountain ranges, canyons and gorges. Mountains over 3,000 metres tall are common. Some of them were formed by mountain-building processes and erosion on land before becoming submerged under the sea. Others have been carved out by under-water currents. Sloping canyons are carved from turbid currents – resembling underwater avalanches – which sweep mud and sand further out to sea. Rivers

wash silt and other sediment out to sea, and this settles at the bottom of oceans.

The continents and ocean basins 'ride' on huge slabs of the Earth's crust called plates. Where the edge of one ocean plate slips under another plate, a deep trench forms. Some of the trenches drop down for more than 10 kilometres. The Challenger Deep in the Pacific Ocean's Mariana Trench, for example, is 10,917 metres deep.

A computer-generated map of the ocean depths

Trenches

△ Ocean trenches form at the edge of the Earth's crustal plates, when one plate pushes under a neighbouring one. Many trenches run roughly parallel to continental coasts.

GOING DOWN

Many factors change with increasing depth in the oceans. Sunlight is only able to penetrate to a depth of about 100 metres, and this area is known as the photic zone. By a depth of about 1,000 metres there is a twilight zone where visibility is reduced to a few metres. No light reaches the bathypelagic zone.

The temperature of the oceans falls with increasing depth. Near the surface, temperature depends mainly on the climate, and it is hotter in the tropics than at the poles. Evaporation and the inflow of river water also affects the surface temperatures. By a depth of about 2,000 metres however, the temperature falls to about 3°C and remains more or less constant. This is because there are few deep currents at this level to mix the water.

Sunlit zone 195m

Twilight zone 990m

Bathypelagic zone 5,850m

Trench zone 18,900m

▽ The ocean is divided into four main zones. Anglers (1) Hatchets (2) Vipers (3) and Photostomias (4) all live in the deep trench zone.

DEEP SEA LIFE

Fish that live in deep water feed mainly on the remains of dead surface animals that sink to the bottom. Some strange fish inhabit the inky blackness of the deepest oceans. Many of them have large mouths which they always keep open as they swim around, looking for prey. Others have luminous spots of light which enable them recognise each other and their neighbours. The various angler fish have a luminous blob at the end of a projection from their heads, which acts as a lure to tempt prey within reach.

A deep sea fish underwater

The sea floor has a varied landscape, and some of the mountains that originate in the sea are tall enough to reach the surface, forming islands. Other islands are formed by the eruption of underwater volcanoes, or from the activity of corals. For example, Hawaii (right) is a chain of volcanic islands in the Pacific Ocean.

▽ Where one crustal plate rides over another, the lower one descends back into the mantle at a subduction zone. Molten rock rising up between two ocean plates creates a mid-ocean ridge.

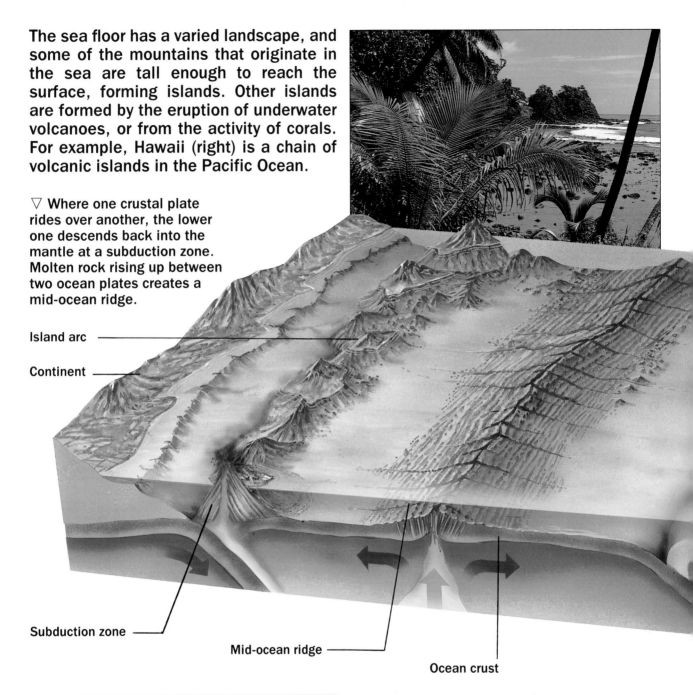

Island arc

Continent

Subduction zone

Mid-ocean ridge

Ocean crust

MID-OCEAN RIDGES

Down the centre of the major oceans, the crustal plates are gradually moving apart. This happens because molten rock from the Earth's mantle constantly wells up between them. As this hot lava cools, it forms a pair of parallel ridges. These are known as mid-ocean ridges. The whole process is called sea-floor spreading, and it causes the plates of the oceans and continents to gradually move apart. The rocks in the ridges are the youngest in the Earth's crust. The Mid-Atlantic Ridge, for example, runs southwards from Iceland along the centre of the Atlantic Ocean, until it curves eastwards to join the Indian Ocean Ridge.

In some places volcanoes rise up to 1,000 metres from the sea bed to form tall, underwater mountains. In shallower parts of the ocean, the volcanoes may even be tall enough to break the surface as islands. Waves may wear away the top of a volcanic island, and such submerged islands are called a flat-topped guyot, or seamount.

REEF FORMATION

Corals are small animals related to jellyfish and sea anemones. They extract a chalky substance, calcium carbonate, from sea water and use it to build their skeletons. When the corals die, their skeletons remain as gnarled rocky growths. Corals live only in well-lit, warm tropical waters no deeper than 60 metres. Near a shore, corals build up to form a fringing reef; further out they form a barrier reef.

Sometimes corals form a fringing reef round a volcanic island. As the volcanic peak is eroded and the sea level rises, the coral continues to grow towards the shallows. Finally the island sinks, leaving a ring of coral known as an atoll. This explains why such islands have deep, cliff-like sides of coral when viewed from underwater.

Trench

Volcano

The Great Barrier Reef of Australia

DID YOU KNOW?

A coral reef is a self-contained habitat for many organisms. The Great Barrier Reef in Australia, for example, is home to over 3,000 different species. In addition to fish, there are crabs, jellyfish, sea anemones, sea cucumbers (which are animals) and starfish. Even the corals themselves are animals.

MAKE AN UNDERWATER VOLCANO

You can mimic the effect of an underwater volcano. Pour cold water into a bucket until it is nearly full. Then fill a small plastic bottle with hot water, adding a few drops of coloured dye. Screw the cap on the bottle and place it at the bottom of the bucket. Now unscrew the cap and watch as the less dense hot water rises to the surface.

Hot water and coloured dye

Bucket

Bottle

Cold water

The water in the oceans is constantly on the move. At the surface, wind whips the sea up into waves that move over great distances. The gravitational pull of the Moon and Sun also causes tides to rise and fall each day. In addition to all these movements, underwater currents shift masses of water round the world.

WAVE MOVEMENT

Waves are caused by an up-and-down movement of water — only when waves break on the shore do they make water move along. The waves are merely large versions of the ripples you see on ponds. You can demonstrate their movement by making a cork float in a pond and dropping a stone into the water near it. As the ripples pass the cork, they make it bob up and down in the same place.

In the open sea, wind starts wave movement. Particles of water circulate immediately under the waves, and at the surface this movement may cause a wave to break, or turn over. Waves can travel over great distances and the distance between wave peaks is known as the wavelength.

Waves that reach the shore change the landscape. They form beaches, erode cliffs and gradually alter shorelines. Waves also carry beach sand away with them into the oceans.

Cliffs, such as these ones at Marsden Bay in England, are eroded by the action of waves.

Shore

Wind direction

Wave movement

△ Wind causes waves to travel through the sea. The main movement of water is up and down, with water particles rotating in circles. Only at the shore does water move along.

Water particles

TIDES

The gravitational attraction of the Moon pulls the waters of the ocean into a bulge, or high tide, when the Moon is directly overhead. Because the Earth rotates on its axis, centrifugal forces acting on the water cause a similar bulge on the opposite side. The Sun's gravity also affects the oceans and the combined effect of all these forces causes the bulge of water to move round the Earth, making the sea level rise and fall as tides.

A different effect called a tidal wave is caused by underwater earthquakes. Tidal waves have very long wavelengths and travel at hundreds of kilometres per hour. As they approach the shore, their height increases to several metres.

Sun

Spring tide

New Moon

Neap tide

Sun

Half Moon

Gravitational pull of Sun
Gravitational pull of Moon
Solar tide
Lunar tide

△ Spring tides occur when the Moon, Sun and Earth are in a straight line and neap tides when they are at right angles.

◁ Tidal waves are caused by underwater earthquakes and get higher towards the shore. They travel very fast and cause severe flooding.

Earthquake

Wave created

Tidal wave

Currents in the surface water of the oceans are caused mainly by the prevailing winds, and the rotation of the Earth makes the currents move to the right of the wind direction (in the Northern Hemisphere) and to the left (in the Southern). The shapes of landmasses and the ocean bed also affects direction.

CIRCULATION

Currents move in a circular pattern and are called gyres. The gyres rotate in a clockwise direction in the Northern Hemisphere, and in an anticlockwise direction in the Southern Hemisphere.

Ocean currents can be divided into two main types: cold currents and warm currents. At certain times of the year there are also drift currents, such as the Gulf Stream which flows across the Atlantic towards Europe during winter. The overall effect of all these currents is to mix the waters of the Earth's oceans.

Another type of mixing occurs when wind blows warm surface water away from a shore. Cooler water from below comes up to take its place in a process called upwelling. The subsurface water often contains nutrients which plant-like organisms feed on. These organisms are then eaten by fish and other sea animals. Such upwelling regions are rich in fish.

➡ Cold currents
➡ Warm currents
➡ Seasonal drift during winter

△ Cold surface currents in the Northern Hemisphere flow generally southwards from the North Pole. In the Southern Hemisphere, the cold water circulates round Antarctica.

A thermograph displays different temperatures of the Gulf Stream

HEAT AND DENSITY

Warm water is less dense than cool water and near the Equator, the Sun warms the water much faster than at the Poles. The salt in ocean water also affects density. As water evaporates from the Mediterranean Sea, it becomes more concentrated in salt, and therefore more dense. Currents of less salty — and less dense — water from the Atlantic Ocean and Black Sea flow in to restore the balance.

The opposite effect takes place in the Baltic Sea of northern Europe. In summer, fresh water from rivers and melting ice flows into the sea and reduces its salinity (and hence density). Then the less dense water at the surface flows southwards, forming a current. At the same time an undercurrent of dense, more salty water flows in to take its place.

Ice flowing in the Arctic Sea

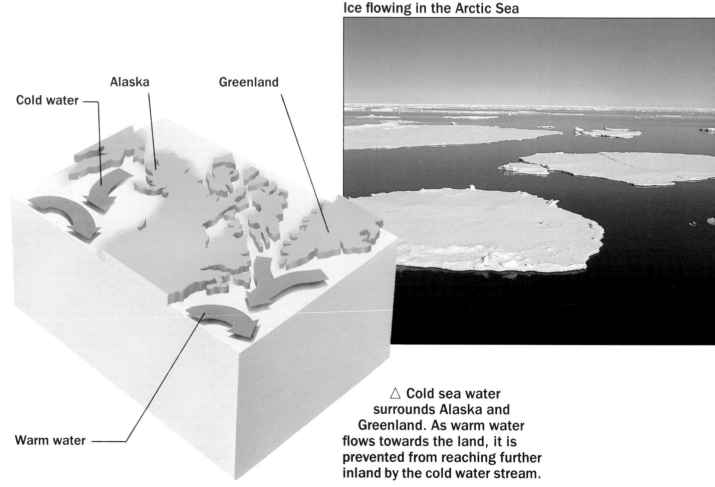

Alaska   Greenland
Cold water

Warm water

△ Cold sea water surrounds Alaska and Greenland. As warm water flows towards the land, it is prevented from reaching further inland by the cold water stream.

Geographers have produced accurate maps of all the world's land surfaces. But over three-quarters of the Earth lies underwater, and we know less about it than we do about the surface of the Moon. The oceans could provide mankind with food and minerals, and are now being intensely studied by scientists.

MAPPING THE SEA BED

Charts of the shallow areas of the ocean have been produced as an aid to navigation for many years. The charts were made using soundings (lowering a weighted rope to measure the depth of the water), and recorded the positions of sandbanks, rocks and other hazards to shipping. Soundings could only be made far out in the ocean if the piece of rope was long enough. However, real progress was not made until the invention of echo-sounding and the development of manned and unmanned submersibles. Then the science of oceanography really took off.

Some equipment used for deep water exploration (1) Sealink (2) Perry chamber (3) Deep sea camera (4) Trieste (5) Box cover (6) JIM and (7) Tech diver

Echo-sounding works by transmitting ultrasonic sound waves to the sea bed and measuring the time taken for the reflected waves to return to the surface. From a knowledge of the speed of sound in sea water, the distance travelled by the sound can be calculated (as well as the depth which is half the total distance). Echo-sounding is similar in principle to the sonar used by submarines for detection and navigation.

Early world map

SUBMERSIBLES

Oceanographers use various devices to explore the sea bed, but the most versatile — and most expensive — is a manned submersible. It is effectively a small submarine built to withstand the tremendous pressures deep in the ocean. Powered by electric motors, a modern research submersible has a pilot and a crew of up to two observers. It carries lights and cameras — including a television camera to send pictures to the surface — and may have robot 'arms' to collect samples from the sea bed.

An alternative method of exploration uses a bathyscaphe. This is a strong, pressurised sphere made of steel. It contains various cameras and instruments. In 1960, two scientists in a bathyscaphe descended nearly 11,000 metres to the bottom of the Mariana Trench in the Pacific Ocean.

▷ The modern submersible has come a long way since the first American submarine. It used hand-operated pumps and propellers.

⑦

⑥

PLUMBING THE DEPTHS

To make a sea-bed map by taking soundings, put gravel and stones in the bottom of a bowl of water. Put some soil in the water and stir. Using a small weight on the end of a piece of string, measure the depth of water above the various features on the bottom and plot the results on a chart.

Mud and gravel

Water

String

Bowl

The oceans are a potential source of minerals for mankind — indeed, many of the mineral deposits found on land were formed originally in the sea. Today's oceans get their minerals in two ways: from minerals dissolved in sea water itself, or from deposits located on or under the sea bed.

DEPOSITS

Minerals extracted from the beds of shallow waters, usually along the off-shore continental shelf, include metal ores of copper, iron, tin and titanium. Some metallic gold can also be found. Non-metallic minerals include phosphates, sulphates, sulphur, shellsand and grit (fine gravel). Rivers that flow through diamond-bearing rocks, such as those off the coast of southwestern Africa, carry alluvial diamonds obtained from the silt and gravel near the river mouths. The minerals are scooped up by dredgers, or pumped ashore along pipes.

Minerals dissolved in sea water are extracted by evaporation — a method used for obtaining salt since ancient times — or by chemical processing. Bromine and iodine, used in medicine and by the photographic industry, are obtained chemically. The chief metal extracted from sea water is magnesium, used for making lightweight alloys.

▽ Many mineral deposits are found just offshore. Rivers flowing through rocks rich in ores wash them into the sea. The ores settle in areas and form deposits.

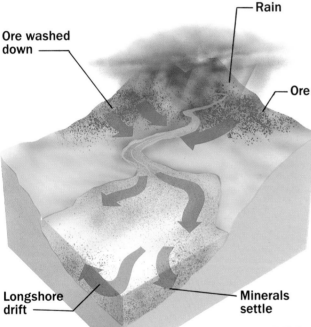

Rain

Ore washed down

Ore

Longshore drift

Minerals settle

▽ The map shows the locations of the chief minerals. Manganese is 'mined' as nodules off the sea bed in deep waters.

○ Gold

▭ Metals
Titanium, Tin, Copper, Iron

▭ Minerals
Shellsands, sulphur
Phosphates, Sand and grit

△ Diamonds

EVAPORATION

In hot parts of the world, people extract salt from sea water by running it into shallow 'pans' and allowing the heat of the Sun to evaporate the water away. You can copy the process by adding salt to a glass or jar of water until no more will dissolve. Pour the salt solution into another glass, and leave it in a warm place, such as near a radiator. As the heat evaporates the water, salt crystals will form.

Evaporating sea water for salt

▽ Oil and gas were formed millions of years ago by heat and pressure, as the bodies of millions of small, dead animals and plants were buried at the bottom of the sea.

OIL AND GAS

Some of the most important minerals found under the sea — in fact under the sea bed — are oil (petroleum) and natural gas. They are important sources of fuels such as kerosene and petrol. They also serve as raw materials for various petrochemical products, ranging from drugs and dyes to plastics and explosives.

These so-called fossil fuels were formed millions of years ago from the remains of creatures that lived in the sea. Normally when a plant or animal dies, bacteria make the remains decay or rot away. But such bacteria need oxygen in order to function, and this was unavailable in the early atmosphere. So the remains fell to the bottom of the sea, where there is little or no oxygen, and different kinds of bacteria worked on them turning them into hydrocarbons. Layers of clay and silt settled over the hydrocarbons, and pressure and heat converted them into oil and gas. The deposits are 'mined' by boring a hole to meet them and piping the product ashore.

Organic matter covered

Heat pressure

Oil and gas trapped in rocks

Fish are a good source of protein, and for centuries they have been caught and used as food by man and other animals. Nowadays fish are also processed in factories to make food for pets and farm animals. Molluscs, such as shellfish and crustaceans (crabs, prawns and lobsters) are also caught for food.

OFFSHORE FISHING

Most of the world's major fishing grounds are in shallow waters near the continents. On the continental shelves, the upwelling of nutrients from cooler, deeper water provides a good feeding habitat for the marine population. About 70 per cent of all commercial fish are caught in the Northern Hemisphere. For example, herrings and cod are netted in the cool Northern Atlantic and sardines in warmer Mediterranean waters. The richest fishing ground in the world lies in the Indian Ocean between Japan and the Philippines.

For a long time, most of the fish caught in the Southern Hemisphere came from the offshore waters of Peru in South America, and the main catch was anchovies. But a new warm sea current disrupted the fishing grounds there.

A modern ocean-going trawler

Fence

Rockwall trap

Fishing rod

Lobster pots

Beach seine

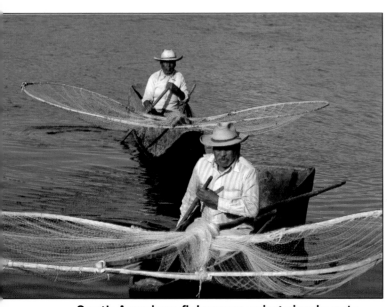

South American fishermen using simple nets

OVERFISHING

Modern fishing vessels are very efficient, and are equipped with a fish-finder (a type of echo-sounder to detect shoals of fish underwater) and two-way radios to receive the latest information about the weather and the location of shoals. But the number of fish in the sea is not unlimited, and there is a danger of overfishing. This means that fish will be caught faster than the stocks are being replaced by breeding.

During the late 1980s, commercial fisheries caught 80 million tonnes of fish each year. Experts believe that with effective international control, the annual catch of all fish, crustaceans and molluscs should never exceed 120 million tonnes. To enforce this maritime nations have territorial waters around their coasts in which no foreign vessel is allowed to fish. Many countries have enlarged these waters to a zone of up to 320 kilometres offshore to protect their fish stocks.

Cast net

▽ Fish may be caught by individual fishermen with rods, small nets or traps, or by groups of men working on boats using trawls, purse seines or gill nets.

Gill net

Lift net

▽ The map below shows the main fishing zones. Fifty per cent of commercial fish are caught along the shores outlined in red.

One of the problems facing the world today is the energy crisis. Fossil fuels (coal, oil and gas) will not last for ever, and even nuclear power can be hazardous.The constant motion of the tides and waves, and the temperature differences in the oceans, are a vast source of untapped energy.

WATER POWER

Waves have a lot of energy. For example during a storm, waves crashing onto the shore are able to demolish sea walls. But how can this energy be harnessed? Two experiments have been set up which rely on the fact that as a wave passes, the water moves up and down. In one experiment a long pontoon, with a sausage-shaped air bag along its upper surface, is anchored out at sea. As a wave passes by, it compresses the air in the bag. The air then works a turbine that drives an electric generator.

A second type of wave-powered generator consists of a long line of pear-shaped floats. Wave action makes them nod up and down, and this movement is again made to drive an electric generator.

Tides are another source of water power. Slow-speed water turbines are placed in a dam across the mouth of a river. These turn as the tide comes in, and turn again as the tide flows out. The water turbines are used to drive electric generators.

Bay of Fundy, Canada

Flexible air bags

Air in

Air out

A Salter's duck at Edinburgh University

△ Experimental projects have been built which harness the energy produced by waves and tides. Wave-powered electric generators have to be located offshore, where they may be a hazard to shipping. Tidal power stations are built on the shore or at the mouths of rivers.

THERMAL ENERGY

Below the comparatively warm surface waters, the temperature of sea water falls rapidly with increasing depth (see page 13). This temperature difference between surface water and deep water can be used to provide energy. In America, a project has been set up called ocean thermal energy conversion (OTEC) to do just that.

The project consists of a floating power station moored in mid-ocean, with a long pipe descending 1,200 metres into the cold water, where the temperature is about 3°C. Pumps lift the cold water up to the power station, where it is used to change ammonia gas into its liquid form. In a heat exchanger, the liquid ammonia is warmed and evaporated back to its gaseous state by warm water from the surface of the sea. The ammonia gas then goes through the same cycle as before. As the liquid ammonia flows around the system, it drives a turbine which generates electricity.

A wave energy machine in Scotland

Living quarters

Wave direction

Warm water

Cold water

DID YOU KNOW?

Unlike fossil fuels, the energy in the oceans is a renewable resource. But how much water is there? The oceans of the world have a combined area of 360 million square kilometres and a total volume of about 1,347 million cubic kilometres.

Because the oceans are so vast, people have been using them as a dumping ground for rubbish, sewage and industrial wastes. Accidental spillages of oil have also added to the pollution. But the long-term effects on wildlife — particularly fish — could have disastrous results for mankind.

THE CHANGING OCEAN

Some of man's activities have an indirect effect on the oceans. Atmospheric pollution and increasing levels of carbon dioxide in the atmosphere (from burning forests and fossil fuels) give rise to the greenhouse effect. This, in turn, can lead to global warming — an overall increase in average temperatures throughout the world. One result of this warming could be melting of the ice at the Poles. The salinity of the oceans would then change and sea levels would rise, flooding huge areas of land.

Dumping of sewage in the sea alters the amount of oxygen and nutrients in the water. Plankton may thrive for a while, but the phytoplankton — the tiny plants that are the ultimate source of food for sea creatures — would die off. This could lead to a mass reduction in marine life.

Plankton blooms off the New Zealand coast

▷ At the end of the last Ice Age the huge ice cap over Scandinavia began to melt. The vast amount of melting water led to a rise in sea levels and later to the formation of the Baltic Ice lake.

———— Baltic lake

☐ Receding ice cap

▨ changing coastline

OIL AND CHEMICALS

Crude oil, either spilled accidentally from ships or dumped deliberately from tankers, is a major threat to the oceans. Spilled oil drifts ashore and ends up coating beaches with a black, sticky mess. It gets into the feathers of seabirds, poisoning them as they try to clean their plumage. Scientists have devised various methods to deal with spillages, but the best approach is to prevent them happening in the first place.

Even more dangerous are the toxic chemicals dumped deliberately into the sea, particularly heavy metals such as cadmium, lead and mercury. During the 1950s and 1960s, Japanese chemical industries dumped 600 tonnes of mercury compounds into Minimata Bay. The chemicals accumulated in fish which were eaten by the local people. Many people became ill and died, and babies were born deformed. This should serve as a sufficient warning, and bring about an international ban on the dumping of any chemicals in the sea.

Cleaning up oil along the coast

PROJECT

One method of dealing with oil spillages is by using detergents. To see how it works, pour a little oil onto some water. Add some liquid detergent, agitate the water, and watch the oil disperse.

Industrial waste being poured into a river

Much remains to be discovered about the oceans. Hundreds of years ago, hardly anything at all was known, and people believed that the Earth was a large, flat island in the middle of a sea with no boundaries. People also thought that the sea was home to various kinds of terrible monsters.

The Kraken is a Norwegian sea monster

An old map, with a flat Earth and monsters

One early belief was the existence of a sea serpent, many metres long. It was supposed to attack ships and devour sailors. The giant squid was also a myth, until dead ones were discovered. We now know that giant squids can grow up to 18 metres long, and propel themselves through the water at 48 kilometres per hour. A giant squid has two long tentacles (and eight shorter ones). People think that it was the huge tentacles that gave rise to the sea serpent myth.

A less fearsome myth concerns the mermaid. Half woman and half fish, it resembles several others from Greek mythology. Mermaids were supposed to sing alluring songs and tempt sailors to their deaths by drowning. Again, an actual creature may have given rise to this myth. The dugong, or sea cow, is a large, plant-eating mammal that lives in the shallow waters off the coasts of Africa, Asia and Australia. It has smooth skin and the females have small breasts, which are thought to resemble those of a woman.

In Greek mythology, the monsters of the deep were supposed to be under the control of the god of the sea, called Poseidon, the brother of Zeus. People believed the monsters were offspring of gods and mortals. Poseidon's counterpart in Roman mythology was Neptune, usually depicted holding a trident and keeping company with dolphins. He is sometimes shown with a man's upper body and a fish's tail, rather like a male mermaid. Dolphins were themselves thought to be derived from men. We now know that after humans, dolphins are the most intelligent mammals.

Mermaids lured sailors to their deaths

Bathypelagic zone
The lowest layer of water in the oceans, with a depth of over 2,000 metres.

Bathyscaphe
A pressurised steel ball in which a person is lowered into the deep ocean.

Cartilaginous
Describing something made of cartilage (gristle), like the skeletons of sharks and related fish.

Continental shelf
The gently sloping sea bed close to the shore of a large land mass, where the sea is shallow.

Euphotic zone
The uppermost layer of water in the oceans, from the surface down to about 150 metres.

Greenhouse effect
Overheating of the Earth's atmosphere caused by a build-up of gases such as carbon dioxide (which prevents heat from escaping into outer space).

Global warming
Gradual increase in the average temperatures throughout the world, possibly as a result of the greenhouse effect.

Guyot
A flat-topped underwater mountain formed from an eroded underwater volcano; also called a seamount.

Hydrocarbon
A chemical compound of hydrogen and carbon; oil (petroleum) and natural gas are hydrocarbons.

Krill
Microscopic shrimp-like animals that live on plankton and provide food for fish and other marine animals.

Mesopelagic zone
The middle layer of ocean water extending from a depth of about 150 metres to 2,000 metres.

Neap tide
A low tide that occurs when the Moon and Sun are at right angles to each other, and their combined gravity pulls on ocean waters.

Phytoplankton
Microscopic plants that form part of plankton.

Plankton
Microscopic organisms that live in or near the surface of the sea.

Salinity
A measure of the saltiness of sea water.

Spring tide
A particularly high tide that occurs when the Moon and Sun are in line, and their gravitational pull acts on the waters in the oceans.

Submersible
A small submarine used for exploring the sea.

Swim bladder
A sac inside the body of a bony fish used to control buoyancy.

Water cycle
The process by which water circulates on Earth. The Sun's heat causes water to evaporate from the surface of the sea as water vapour. This rises into the atmosphere forming clouds as it cools. Over land, clouds release rain which run into rivers, finally flowing back to the sea.

Photographic Credits:
Cover and pages 15, 16, 24 bottom, 26 top and 29 bottom: Spectrum Colour Library; page 5: Eye Ubiquitous; pages 7, 12, 17, 19, 23, 26 bottom, 27 and 28: Science Photo Library; pages 8, 13 and 29 top: Frank Spooner Pictures; page 11 top and bottom: NHPA; page 14: J. Allan Cash Photo Library; page 18: National Maritime Museum Picture Library; page 20: Topham Picture Source; pages 21 and 24-25: Bruce Coleman Limited; page 30 top left: The Hulton Picture Company; page 30 top right and bottom: Mary Evans Picture Library.

PRINTED IN BELGIUM BY
proost
INTERNATIONAL BOOK PRODUCTION